anima

anima

Mario Petrucci

ISBN: 978-0-9573847-3-6

Scan QR code for further title information

Copyright © Mario Petrucci, 2013
www.mariopetrucci.com

Cover photograph © Eleanor Bennett, co-edited by Mario Petrucci
www.eleanorleonnebennett.zenfolio.com

First published May 2013 by:

Nine Arches Press
Great Central Studios
92 Lower Hillmorton Rd
Rugby, Warwickshire
CV21 3TF

www.ninearchespress.com

Printed in Britain by:
imprintdigital.net
Seychelles Farm,
Upton Pyne,
Exeter
EX5 5HY
www.imprintdigital.net

anima

Mario Petrucci

Nine
Arches
Press

for Manjusri

"Reminiscent of e.e. cummings at his best", **Mario Petrucci**'s work is "vivid, generous and life-affirming" (*Envoi*). His most recent poems, inspired by Black Mountain and hailed as "modernist marvels" (*Poetry Book Society*), embrace contemporary issues of profound social and personal relevance via a distinctive combination of innovation and humanity. Through groundbreaking residencies, poetry films and a remarkable output of ecopoetry, his unique scientific sensibility has illuminated the linguistic as well as emotive resonances of love and loss in the public and private domains. Whether exploring the tragedies of Chernobyl (*Heavy Water*, 2004) or immersing himself in heart-rending invention (*i tulips*, 2010), Petrucci aspires to "Poetry on a geological scale" (*Verse*).

CONTENTS

"I fall, have fallen, for that One
hidden within you."

Hafez

*(author's version of a rendering
by Daniel Ladinsky)*

ride the blue lion

which does not buck
as the horse or kick at upward-
going dust with the mule

but draws across that
face too beautiful for contemplation
claws ferocious to

smear crimson rough
with rougher tongue – muscularly
hidebound in fur

-flesh unmannered
versus what animal mind bends
from its place less

mended by down
-ward light or greener for
blood will maul

its bind against
blood or through till
fingers curl

within that
mane & the lion
bluely blind

rampant in
thought cools
couchant

halves

the blade drops
& both half-oranges
rock upon their backs as

beetled species made
zestful but without
the frantic legs

enlarged in heat
to overbrightly dribble
sap in that broken moment

after insect sex which could be
love yet dictates each rolls
apart to undercarriage

straight-grained ex
-posed in falling apart
where one gains access

to tarter matters animal
or vegetable softly to
be consumed for

rind is hard on us
unscooped or what
the starveling leaves

behind or am I for
getting I was once in
heart fruit-perfect & un-

halved?

branched

body
weathers burn
till hurt launched inward knots

brown through grain as if the human
tree could not grow without
some spot

or pain
were fruit & never
knowing what lovely hand should

pick it – so envy oak which clearly
stands simply to endure
climate

while I
blink beneath the brolly
or trot down slopes dodging cloud

-borne shade scudded over grass as
though sun or land were not
what one

thinks
lodged in mind but
all that lasts keen to offer expansive

sand with my only chance to drop
through dark I made or
am

to fall
heavier than any
fruit between what leaves to em-

brace & know my bark as breezing
grace might prompt not
so much

the crop
as fingers in their
earthbound glove to receive

that greenly downward
-going hand of
love

deep the sad things

are that way
the child-body sees
how a word

brings world
leaping & so plays each
again through

black-blood
arteries wending mindflesh
to seethe with

all matter just
beneath visible skin a throb at
temple wrist &

ankle intenser
than ebbing pleasure which moves
slacker to heart

where regret is
felt with all the years an art behind it
richly definite &

that hand reaching
in goldfish light never comes just that
beat in the black

making subtle
sound conjure further black though
nothing lacks

in what is
faced & no joy wished until
unsadness

takes its place

for Pablo Neruda

today my life you

fell through me – light no longer subject
to longing or dismay as if dusks & dawns
had melled then recombined – one object
sight purifies in just that way a bloom

in darkness is no less for never being seen
as I am held in deeper swoons daytimes blur
knowing flowed-through nows come clear
in fragrance nocturnes prise – even mine –

too late to dam the river your perfume swings
vastly & by night over my steep levee – or stem
those aromatics your upward-flowing lingering
fingers climb Muscat-wise through brain –

through bright sleep I groaned for others to make
awakening – in time your waters flood my water slaking
blood depthless in fervent – till we embrace & glory be
you lower yourself relentlessly light gently upon me

See: Cien sonetos de amor (XLIX)

the machine

step into the machine
they said
& we can take you back

undo each & all regret
the girls the booze that bank
I said

the catch?
that's for you to choose they said
just get in first &

take it
step by step so I could have had (I
mean could have)

Margaret? *no –*
better than that the clearest pearl you
never met a flower

a-swirl in mead but
hurry now this power is
expensive & what of illness? mine? *no*

need for that you'll be shown
where you mustn't live look – an open
door sign

here (I cursed) was she then
the one? *of many friend* you mean
rather than the one I

took? you're sure? *oh*
much more than you can know so
meet that hearse

with a silken heart take another
throw...(I'd one leg
in) I said

&
what about
my son?

your son? ah
– nothing to be done nothing
we can do but

there'll be others just like
him & not unkilled & he'll never know
you know   nor you

I know
now I said (they began to fret the floor
began to slide) *we need*

answers get
inside don't make this your biggest
yet I

saw a face
somewhere still at play a door
swept shut

then
disappeared as I whispered
through air distilled

I'll stay

19

as clouds at

times
hold a cloud
to make us

dwell
till something sly
in vapour

-swirl
fixes : lets us
glimpse

what
clouds are – so
it is

when i
sense how flesh
unmixed

can yield
this heart in
yours

& life in
fluid
apartness

seizes
&
all I is

held

for Pablo Neruda ('Tonight I Can Write…')

because i have

lost her I hold her gaze in mine
who never loses who sees me under
the bone moon bones in her eyes daze

all love shown in singlest glance nothing
survives other than love what eyes
steady behind a look covered

recovered as one loses a stone
generations passed down on single
fingers regenerations to regain her I

found because I looked & all gazing salt who
think eyes that dance lose translating
flesh to other flesh that thinned

mink a thumbtip brushed in her small
of back or animal between thighs made
heady muse what is never held I cannot

lose as oceans do not hold the dolphin ever
passing through I have her now who
passed in trueness feel her

glide within as certain days become
asides to time as though I were that air emp-
tied leap-stunned over water what waters hide

after dolphins

cloud again

won't leave
blue alone : loud
undersides

bright
-hueing east – that
dullness

west
so what if this mind
is

sky
to cloudthought
not

at all
its kind but
beyond

what
thought moves in
&

behind
that in which each
moves

as space is
breath *through* self
that makes

static
blue where i
take

thought
for cloud
cloud

for sky
&
sky

you

gem

wets
flesh &
fluxes blood in

glow
a stab unseen
so greenly within its

dark
life-stark in
contrast to bone whose

muscles
hem & know
though no flood this

one
-beaded
dew shone fast &

held
where none
other

is –
that glint in
love through red &

black
as gold in a
drawer caught up in

a ring
curves back
& back to find its

flaw
until it
sets with you

the stone

for Adam

how you move

zagged
within as if
what is sky or

blue in me had fallen
for earth & with
no

dialect nor
direct approach
resolved to descend

branch-wise then climb
again through this
adam or eve

each life
each love a foot
-hold towards greener

light : speech the bud
-soft knot in
throats

that bark & rot in
divinity you
left me

&
sounds
the heart's now

makes
you place one
by one as leaves upon

the tree

i could say this

blue
sky-perfect were
a blue

bowl –
true ghost of sapphire
or invert

ghost of
pacific – though another
said so

with wisdom
to sit beneath it alert as she
spoke

for whom thought
is no
firmament but a choir or this

early summer
bled through later autumn her
manner of

sleeping to
winter such that her She in me
inclined

inwardly
unblind resembles how an eye
may bless

skies with
-out fault or dream the being
constant

to one
self as breathing is or when
bodies

flounder
then halt that constancy
yet more

extreme
undeathly breath has
found

in breathlessness

sapphire

for whom
there is no stone
in me

as though
looming seas had tried
to fill her

one drop
but stopped unable leaving
themselves

less pure &
too alone or sky had been
richer once

whose crows
blew across beautiful as
the necessary

flaw her
stone set in white or
gold must

point to
without being as
she becomes

light-old
mettle whose
blue

-crystal
grits facet
by facet

accrue
&
settle

there is

in a man
that woman who
grows him – flower

from his niche whose
towered rocks
tick

heat
to narrow
his gap a life

each weather hers
her petals
his

a means
for light to
prise past &

show the stamen
shame men
stumble

into
boozy as
bees with yellow

-specked regret
dusting legs
japanned

listless
in seeming
flight unaware

even when wing-
heavy resolve
allows &

hard in
-sect alights
how it is the bloom

that flies

when ocean

comes to
a face hot with
salt & swells behind

eyes where
no one sees as if
pacific or arctic worked

their weight
entire to deliver
the lover the palmful tears

in erosions
those endless sands
down cheeks through veins

insane with
parting the only
grief as beloveds release

voice in
singled embrace
one cry as the gull just

now
dropped under
skies seizing air or

waves
break for
rest in restless

spume
on shores
where once

again
each to
each dis-

solves
grain a-
gainst

grain

as same

there is
the hand to which a hand
is glove

or love
on which each saner love
is skin

& skins
that brush furthest reaches
or reach

far within
a woman through whom
the girl

once
walked for all her pain
a man

under
half a moon finding
her

hand
again unfurls him
so

greenly
yellow & rain
less as

single
blooms in
sand

V

overhead
soundless
almost

that
swish &
squeak

of feathered
air
subtle-rush

wings
the wobbled
necks

so near
one
rear-straggler

full-spanned
with
a flicker

merest
shudder
realigns

& already
gone
they have

shifted
blueness
moved

through
then on
now

made
effortless
yet

utterly
heavily
present

as you

room

within
none ever
walked through

walls
unpainted with chords
yellowed

beneath silt
& caught between brick
each ability

to weep
bedded in plaster to cover
notes as

if music
were indicant absence for
what

instruments
never express though this
covert man

is able
sat by a window black
with lateness

halved
in love for all quiets
he cannot

hear
quite pianissimo
through

night
artful with dawn all on
its brink

agape
with the next his very next
beat b-

rushing
that rim outermost in him
ever after

about to
return even as it burns
lock to

key
in the one his
undone

heart

intervals

not
what is
or isn't but

every
absence
separately

made
itself in
what fits

round
or nudges
to it for each

thing
happens
as friction be

-tween
something &
nothing comes

to you
humbly in
– no – *as* your

dark be
-fore you
knew dark

wrong
or dark's
nature could

be
your own
& only light

known
forever in
whatever one

thought
one hadn't
had (would

never
have) &
therefore

was
all
along

anima I

cannot write
her straight – this
man in whom straightness is

an arrow curving
its path : mere illusion
for lovers who plot where it arcs

I cannot know
her in this line I draw
back tauter than the string that lets

pain go or
the bow supple in its
bend yet ever prone to warp & send

off-true : so
how may I find a You
where speech is impossible unless

this skimming
of targets be the way
into speaking between a man &

that woman he
started with neither
mother nor wife but She he

squints at
clear through near
-sighted morning as if

her stroke
steady & precise
through him were

all
air ready
to be parted

nearness of lovers

tight on the Tube
so
close the soft thrust

of the train bitters my
lip
on the twill of his right

shoulder
i smell the second waft
of her

breathed
aroma white with tended
teeth

reserved
for him received by this
stranger

who suddenly loves
before
her beau can

that wateriness
in blue
as her still

eyes
unblock something
of me

through him
&
i hear in thunder

wheels upon wheels
his
small gasp to the rock

of her carriage : words
intended
for one nuzzled other

urgency spills as
love
does – as love

does

& i turn

find you
in each formal
guise : mother daughter

wife crone – unrequited
in yourself & so
you

seek
me many-eyed
hand trailed thumb-first

where life pinches till
loins thicken as
soft bone

i
must yield to
bring another hand & an

other unflinching : Shakti
rapt with Shiva
at her

centre
our tender tap
-root healed whose

darkest innermost sep-
arable thread i
am

&
what sap
now rises to leaf or

flower
ever unseen
unsaid in the field

bonfires

begun
in me : my wan
sun relocates to many-billioned

earth & waters through head then
heart bone each moment
narrows to

marrowed
pyre writhing flame
as hip & cheek in upwards slaps

of ignition whose wisps thinly
lipped in indecision must
come again

aspiring
smoke that is old
wood taken in breath to

breath even as it warms
ash left in pans
or this

Novembered
life that takes a hand
of the woman met once wet

with dream become incendiary
-pure who stands in
man in

particular
me to rekindle
ages – her shape

I staged in imagined
nightly flesh now
launched

manifest
within into what was
darkly manless flight : undefused

she sparks beyond human reach
erupts my darkened
wests &

easts one
by one to each
beat in my chest those

perfect scorching breasts

how that

night I
walked colonnades
from alga fountain to private stucco

paving
gently inclined to
departure with pitch-perfect fireworks

over &
shrill arias closed
my one cappuccino seized in me I ran

lovers
in gamuts in coved
pairs & fours engrossed in hair &

cheek
young sailors at
landed mermaids wan-faced

with love
or semblance
wobbled up from titanic

waters they
goggled through
sleek with lust or odd

affection
at this passer-
by casually ignored as

only one
unloved with eyes
betraying frisson at my

audience
casual as a wake
I trailed on forsaken sea

to turn
in pitch a single
key stiffly blind yet held

in fragrant
dark I glimpsed
how stars to me were

closest thing
to cries uncried
& starriness mostly

empty
then came
within a breath a

trance
of thinking
that though neither

of us
then knew &
might never know some

where likewise illumined
by dark & stars in
whatever

company you were you
glanced up suddenly
alone &

saw them too

how   animal s-

urges blood
through this body
body cages whose tenderest

thumbtip becomes claw where
faintest brush en-
roars

the man
a pelt gored from
within by mind a scuffle

between small & desperate
lives heard close yet
vague on

a forest floor
otherwise hushed : oh
send in the archer to descend

each bump & knoll of my spinal
pass without rifle or
fire but

a back
more supple &
divining than any rod for

creatures too long stunk in
endless mire who
ruffle &

part cover
towards unmothering
hands as if the huntress distinct

through eastern fog unslung from
one quivering shoulder
her reddest

godmost
heart where every
unculled beast that comes

could lull & drink

your fragrance

steals all other
perception
stills a man with

skin & breath that
rise
together in singular

aroma whose dank
forest
so delicately ancient

lit by off-white stars
striped
in black-green space

says – o mars look to
this
keen-eyed venus lithe

within you & crouched
behind
your well-tooled ways

see enshadowed one who
plays
under moons older more

lustrous than manly gold
unsunned
your tigress dew-heavy

in undergrowth tense
as rippled
rock with sheathed

claw seeks a mate
softly
knocks down as

supple weight
you
who have not

yet believed
through
loss in her

every sense

O anima

you ran
ahead when magma
was just a girl hurled along masculine

vertebrae to spill her tresses hotly orange
or part in pleasure there &
here her

many yellow
lipsticked mouths – you
blessed the pool where bacteria unthinking

Brownian ways through measured light chose
instead one day to walk &
continents

still fused
hip to shoulder you
smouldered on each southern bed dreamy

with depth & loosely loved where underwater
vents teethed in druse sent
upwards

plumed
biota as campfires do
by gloomy streams & even through reptilian

doom you grew patient for me as the Nile for
sand or that green-brown rind
on crocodiles

you waited
for sun & mind to grow me
with every journey hearse-to-crib become one

slow breath & now i breathe creation in
as though that oxygen were
easy on

these lungs
received through a look
fearlessly ancient from a creature formed

not of rib but water who found at last air &
fire or as bluish Earth in
all its seas

glares in love
upon airier blues or the air
-borne bird ever chooses to keep motionless

its egg or settles in the nest it makes itself
with delicate shivers to rest
within

that perfect
fit – though today i sleep &
skit so sense myself a swallow stalled &

brought too soon to ground who sees thus
calls to your sky moving on
above to

wait for me

for Hafez

when sun low

white
turns purest
light ice for there are

times slight warmth
chills so
i

mind
love's slow
round : her circles in

-complete within which
bind & wheel
yet

seem in a woman's
eyes to rise
O

there have been moons
as would smother
tides

& palms upon me
coolly bridal
turned

endlessly
from breath to
dark the sunbound

body
barely sees
whose beams impinge

on cue
as sun turns
to bleating earth &

leans
never asking
Look – what in heat you

took
from me & i
in love have done for

you

for Hafez

how did

love
start love
in me? these petals

made filigree in wind
thinly mattered
a rose

nothing
if not the rose &
that yellow heart where it

happens first then hips
blushed later
burst

in exposure though no
white bud or
lip

is
ever fearful
nor fearless quite tinged

stubborn
to each extremity
with knowing rust's intensity

heart-held flowers one either
must cling to or
open

for Hafez

how our stars

fall to heaven not
up
from hell: twinned

flares unseen in op-
position
that dare cross them

selves across the sea
-through
moon in soundless omen

a quick amen in bodied sky
light
swells to bluest child these

plutonic cells uncurtailed
&
indivisibly double this

zygote afternoon that
brings
to hours made all

but ionic with
bright
electrics our

invisibly
parallel
filaments

of night

for Hafez

for nothing is not

the lover
bestowing : this
clasp of light in mind

the billion embraces each
hot eye takes in its
world –

so i look
to you as though
the looking were some finding of

love in itself & that fullest bind &
grasp of love what makes
beloveds

unfurl

small love poem

& all the big things
half-said

their immense machineries
seized

the state with its tense angels
pleased

till none sings except in dread
i ask

instead what love cannot say
yet

gleans as heart's squat flask
yields

illimitless in & out in
fist

-sized gulps of
world

seas

body

in whose softest temples
self holds hosts
aloft

for doubting blood to
witness its own
resurrection

that woman in me
who serves to
overturn

each sexless icon
yet no nerve
here or

touch congregates
unless stars
first

align mote-dust sins
to caress them
selves

bared where small fault
lies in that sanctum
the lived

life makes love to either
its own beat or sp-
urned

as i at last ask mothering
skin what flesh or
limb

could burn itself or in
bodily offering be
so burnt

by the now-untied
god-heated
heart?

these bodies

making
others appendage
to desire

her stretched
fingers all mine now
his brain brass

-blocked right
here envied or pressed
into : my ring

-mark in her
wax bosom – fist-clench
in his

solar
schedules & all along that
longed-for

disembodiment
to never suffer consequence
yet if

in love
i clicked knuckles tactile
within her

cleft hair or
ran feet cloven though
his darkening

simper
might that man that
woman in

me
recognise at last
enough

to meet?

when light grazes

low &
white a winter
bloom

not
too hot to gaze at
not

quite
itself but dropped a
moon

almost
this sun that woman
within

her
blown circle perfect
in pursuit

an arc
scent-close bent on
pollination

one
to one her hair's
corona

wiry
dark drenched
over

skin
between
limbs

as i
half-open to
her

petalled choice
testing
its only spring to

find
among these parts
at last

unclenched & into
tart
& yellow-centred

mind
how old how still
love

teeming crisp in
seeming
cold above its

farthest
rim can lift
&

whisper

for Walt Whitman

questions

draw no faith-sap but
earth
massive in her opera

of mineral & element
springs
my brimmest fruit so

sour in sweetness so
sweet
through acid these

teeth a currency
stripped
to blood & care

set one tongue at
cavities
joyously unknown to

eyes eloquent beyond
sight
that hungers for body

its fat root taps to
make
throat a manner of

loins whose hot jet
words
the unevasive act &

have i been sufficient
or
returned in singled gaze

more than hers this earth
-woman
look entering what is emp-

tied as if heart's flesh might
be
more than chamber or pump

but a thumped recognition
again &
again behind semblance

each fall & rise subtle
beneath
larger breath when

breathing speaks
&
is that message

endless in heat she
unminds
in me so clearly these

fresh shoots tender in
my green
are potent for light

blood knows

no
woman
or man only

now's
need to flow
though all ceases

so in
appearance
before these lovers

flushed
within me as
male / female grown

thin with
world can clot
the woman-wound my

doubter
ever fingers or
in breath bled between

lips that
clamp-clasp at
last as fulsome muscle

the protagonistic gasp
-together instant
only to

part again over
full-stopped
black

& red
with loving
dread on a sheet

rinsed in the east
until my night
resolves

so
all genders
creased in light

&
lost to lack
dissolve

as woman

enters
man anima
-lly you come hot

with yourself in thrusts
beyond blood in
me

cells brim
what mind-rust
cannot unsurge through

lungs as singled shr-
ill in spirited
gull

heavily
winged yet
equalled on air

love's tall flight & its
shadow instinct
-shaped

slung
beneath you
light-flapped & mine

spilled to stall me even
as you wrap
me

in myself

today

the beech
has womanly hair
greened in the long wind

that wise you sway in me
apart from the array
though no

casual eye
could discern how
bark may be male cast upon

womanliness or root stern
mirror to the man
branchless

again yet
on his small way
in steps of seed as mast

launched on feminine air
while rain swept in
fast &

hard is
the lover's gaze
unregarded through glassless

panes where your eyes become
mine about to weep
sight

wracked
deeper than laughter
when two meet under solar

sameness : your moon to my
sun my sun in brighter
blackness

as you
make of day's dark
no lack but light at length

my north back to its
south with this
man by

woman
held vast &
free until either

death or
endless breath again so
i can

breathe
my last into your
tender

mouth